Records Management

Steven M. Bragg

AccountingTools®

ISBN 978-1-64221-172-6

For more information about AccountingTools® products, visit our Web site at www.accountingtools.com.

Table of Contents

About the Author

Steven Bragg, CPA, has been the chief financial officer or controller of four companies, as well as a consulting manager at Ernst & Young. He received a master's degree in finance from Bentley College, an MBA from Babson College, and a Bachelor's degree in Economics from the University of Maine. He has been a two-time president of the Colorado Mountain Club, and is an avid alpine skier, mountain biker, and certified master diver. Mr. Bragg resides in Centennial, Colorado. He has written more than 300 books and courses, including *New Controller Guidebook*, *GAAP Guidebook*, and *Payroll Management*.

Steven maintains the accountingtools.com web site, which contains continuing professional education courses, the Accounting Best Practices podcast, and thousands of articles on accounting subjects.

Buy Additional AccountingTools Courses

AccountingTools offers more than 1,500 hours of CPE courses, with concentrations in accounting, auditing, finance, taxation, and ethics. Related courses that you might like include:

- Accounting Controls Guidebook
- Accounting Information Systems
- Accounting Procedures Guidebook
- The Year-End Close

Go to accountingtools.com/cpe to view these additional courses.

AccountingTools®

Chapter 1
Records Management Overview

Introduction

Every business creates many types of records. A record is stored information used as evidence and information, and which has value by being retained for a certain period of time. The more obvious examples are invoices arriving from suppliers or being sent to customers, each one designed to specify the amount owed by the recipient. There are many other types of records, such as:

- *Cash receipts*. A receipt is given to a customer who pays with cash or a credit card.
- *Customer contracts*. Companies enter into formal contracts with their suppliers and customers, detailing the terms and conditions of sales agreements.
- *Customer records*. A company maintains an ongoing accounts receivable record of the billings issued to a customer and the amounts that the customer has paid to the company.
- *Employee manuals*. A company creates an employee manual, which sets forth all employee-related policies and employment issues.
- *Meeting minutes*. The board of directors keeps minutes of its meetings, detailing the decisions made and actions taken at each meeting.
- *Remittance advices*. A customer prints a check to pay for an invoice, and mails in both the check and a remittance advice that details which invoices are being paid.
- *Tax returns*. A business compiles tax returns, as well as the working papers used as the basis for the information in the tax returns.
- *Time cards*. An employee completes a time card that lists her hours worked each day, and submits it to the payroll department, which will convert it into a payment.
- *Titles to property*. An organization may have title documents for any land, buildings, vehicles, and so forth that it owns.
- *Webinars*. A company creates a video presentation that is conducted over the Internet, with interaction from participants via videoconferencing. A record of this event may be retained.

In each of these situations, a record of some kind is created as part of the ongoing operations of a business.

In this chapter, we address the need for and problems with records, the records life cycle, and several related topics.

The Need for Records

Why does a business need to create and maintain records? There are a number of reasons, including the following:

- *Regulatory compliance.* The applicable government authorities may require that certain records be kept. For example, an environmental protection agency might require that records be kept of the purchase, storage, and use of hazardous materials. Or, a company is required to maintain vehicle registration information for its fleet of service vehicles.
- *Tax compliance.* The government operates from tax receipts, and so requires that records be kept for the compilation and submission of tax payments. This can include sales and use tax records, as well as the working papers needed to compile an income tax return.
- *Operations.* Records are a key part of the operations of a business; they are needed as documentation of which process steps have already taken place, and which ones are still to be completed. For example, a labor routing provides information about which types of labor are needed at each step of the production process in order to create a product.
- *Financial reporting.* A business summarizes information from its accounting records into a set of financial statements. These records may be audited to ensure that the financial results of a business are accurate.
- *Evidence.* Records may be needed as evidence in a legal dispute, to support the claims of the organization.

In short, records are a core requirement of any organization, both to ensure that it functions properly, and also to be in compliance with regulatory and tax requirements.

Problems Related to Records

Why is records management such an important topic? Because a business can be severely impacted if its records management system does not function properly. For example:

- *Record access problems.* Records may be mis-filed, lost, or hoarded by employees. No matter what the reason may be, not having immediate access to records interferes with the proper completion of tasks, which can delay deliveries, impinge on customer service issues, and delay the issuance of financial statements.
- *Record destruction problems.* Records may be incorrectly destroyed. When this involves title records, a business may have difficulty selling off its assets. Lost records may also result in negative legal judgments if the organization was not retaining records in accordance with the relevant laws.
- *Record storage costs.* There may be no system in place for deciding which records to retain, and for how long. In this situation, a business may spend an

inordinate amount to store records that it no longer needs. This situation can also impede operations if records are clogging operational areas.

- *Document discovery.* When a business is subjected to a lawsuit, all records relevant to the case must be identified and retrieved from storage. This *discovery* process can be painfully expensive, especially when the records to be accessed include a broad range of items for which there is no clear records management policy, such as e-mails, spreadsheets, internal memos, blogs, and podcasts.

Given these concerns, we will use the rest of this book to create a path to a better records management system that will support an organization's goals, rather than impede them.

Types of Records

Traditionally, all records involved printed documents, essentially relying on the printed word to convey information. This is no longer the case. Now, records management covers a much larger range of record types, including audio and video recordings. Also, text-based information may never be printed. Instead, e-mails and text messages may originate in electronic format and be stored that way. Storage media may include cloud storage, compact discs and photographs, as well as outmoded storage media such as microfilm.

The general concept of different types of records can be broken down into several sub-categories of records. One way to view record types is by sorting them into internal and external record classifications, as follows:

- *Internal records.* These records are needed to operate a business. For example, a customer sales order, purchase requisitions, inventory control records, and shipping authorizations are needed to produce and ship goods to a customer.
- *External records.* These records contain information that is intended for use outside of the entity. Examples are company newsletters and public relations news releases.

Another way to sort records is within the preceding classification of internal records, but at a finer level of detail, where we break them down into the transaction and reference record classifications, as follows:

- *Transaction records.* These records are used in the conduct of a firm's daily operations. A transaction record is most commonly either a paper-based or electronic form. These records are created via forms, since they involve high-volume transactions that must be standardized as much as possible in order to achieve high levels of efficiency. Examples are sales orders, purchase orders, and shipping documents.
- *Reference records.* These records are used to support operational decisions that occur at longer intervals than ongoing daily operations. They are typically

referenced to determine how a situation was handled in the past. Examples are the corporate travel policy, the employee manual, and the corporate strategy document. Reference records can also provide a history that can be used as the basis for future decisions. Examples are price lists and financial statements.

Record Retention Criteria

Each type of record must be examined to determine its level of use to the organization. This review can then be used to develop a record retention policy that assigns different levels of protection and retention to different types of records. Possible criteria to use for this examination are as follows:

- *Required for core business operations.* Examples are articles of incorporation and bylaws, property titles, shareholder lists, and court settlement documents.
- *Necessary for general business operations.* Examples are customer contracts, purchase records, sales records, and personnel records.
- *Helpful but not essential for general business operations.* Examples are memos sent to employees regarding policy changes, customer correspondence, and legal correspondence.
- *No additional use once their initial usage period has passed.* Examples are routine e-mails among employees and voice mail messages.

Once records have been sorted with these criteria, they can be slotted into a records category. Each of these categories is assigned a different document storage and retention priority. For example:

- *Essential records.* These records are stored in the most secure environment, and are retained in perpetuity. Records required for core business operations are most likely to receive this designation.
- *Important records.* These records are placed in a safer storage environment, and assigned a reasonably long storage interval. Records classified as necessary for general business operations are most likely to receive this designation.
- *Useful records.* These documents are placed in general storage, and given a reasonable retention period before being destroyed. Records classified as helpful but not essential are most likely to receive this designation.
- *Nonessential information.* These documents may not be classified as records, so no attempt is made to store them. This classification may cover the bulk of all information that a business generates.

The Record Life Cycle

Every record progresses through a life cycle, starting with its origination and ending with its destruction. How a record is handled varies in this life cycle, depending on the record retention criteria that have been applied to it. The basic steps in the record life cycle are as follows:

1. *Creation.* A record may be created internally, or received from an outside source. For example, a purchase order arrives from a customer, while a purchase requisition is created internally.
2. *Application.* Once created or received, the information in the record is applied. For example, when a purchase order is received from a customer, the record is applied by sending it to the sales staff, which logs the order and creates an internal sales order that will then be used to create and ship goods.
3. *Retention.* Once the information in a record has been applied, it is stored within a physical or electronic storage system. In addition, there may be several iterations of record retrieval, where a request is made to pull the record from storage, after which it is stored again.
4. *Disposition.* There are two phases within the disposition step. After a period of time, records may be shifted to a lower-cost form of long-term ownership. Also, after the designated retention period has passed, they are disposed of via record destruction. It is also possible that essential records are maintained in perpetuity, and so will avoid this last step.

Record Formats

Paper-based (physical) records continue to be the de facto standard form of record, since they do not require special equipment to read, and are easily annotated. However, physical records can be mis-filed and require a considerable amount of storage space; also, younger generations are now more accustomed to reading electronic documents. Consequently, it is reasonable to assume that physical records will comprise a decreasing proportion of all records.

The record format that will likely surpass physical records is electronic records. These records are permanently stored on many types of media, including storage discs, personal computer hard drives or solid state drives, business servers, and cloud server farms. These records can be accessed by querying the storage device, which means that the same record can potentially be accessed by multiple people in multiple locations at the same time – which is a major advantage over the use of physical records.

Another advantage of electronic records is that they support the use of a distributed work environment. It is quite possible, if not advantageous, for a business to allow its employees to work from home, thereby eliminating their commute times and enhancing employee satisfaction. This arrangement is made possible by the use of electronic record storage, so that each employee can readily access the information they need from a central server.

A cross-over record format that lies between physical records and electronic records is document imaging. This is a document scanning, indexing, storage, and retrieval system that scans paper documents and stores the image in an electronic format. The information in these images can be converted into text with optical character recognition (OCR) software, at which point the information can be considered a purely electronic record.

Information Governance

Information governance is the system of policies and procedures that provides structure to a records management system. These policies and procedures are intended to ensure that there is compliance within an organization throughout the record life cycle for all types of records.

The policies and procedures that comprise an information governance system are promulgated by a committee that is comprised of relevant managers and users from across an organization. These representatives are likely to come from the following areas:

- *Records management*. This group is most directly impacted by information governance, since it is either directly or indirectly responsible for records management.
- *Information technology*. Many policies and procedures require the active assistance of the information technology group, since they are responsible for electronic record storage.
- *Legal*. The legal team is concerned with the legal requirements for storing and accessing records, and so can provide advice on the duration of records storage and the most useful record retrieval methods.
- *Accounting*. The accounting department is the largest producer and user of records within an organization, and so has a large stake in the nature of all records management policies and procedures.

The Records Management System

Records management is the systematic administration of records for their entire life cycle, beginning with their creation or receipt and extending through their classification, use, filing, retention, storage, and eventual disposition. The concept is sometimes extended to include the management of information, which is known as records and information management.

The system used to manage records is a complex amalgamation of a number of factors that must work together in concert. When it works properly, a records management system should flawlessly process each step in the record life cycle. The building blocks of this system include the following:

- *Policies and procedures*. There must be a records management plan, as well as a supporting set of policies, procedures, forms, and training programs that are all designed to minimize error rates while maximizing the efficiency of the records management system.

- *Personnel.* Employees must be properly trained in the policies and procedures of the records management system, so that they can routinely engage in each activity in the record life cycle. There must also be a review system in place for evaluating the records management performance of employees; this may lead to enhanced training for some personnel, and the replacement of others.
- *Equipment.* There must be adequate storage systems for both physical and electronic records that balance the offsetting issues of cost and record accessibility.

The Records Manager

The person responsible for records storage within a business is the records manager. This position is responsible for the proper indexing, storage, retrieval, and security of all records within an organization. This is a key position in a larger organization, where there may be an ongoing demand for proper records management in order to deal with the vast amount of information being generated. The following are key responsibilities of the records manager:

- Ensure that all legal obligations are met for creating and retaining records.
- Ensure that storage indexes are correctly formulated and applied to documents, as well as to the boxes in which they are stored.
- Ensure that all permanent files and confidential records are segregated and properly protected from damage.
- Oversee all aspects of the document storage area, including its layout, security, and protections against fire and water damage.
- Ensure that requested documents are promptly retrieved from storage and delivered to the requesting parties.
- Formulate and enforce restrictions on record access, including the approvals required for document retrieval.
- Periodically conduct a comprehensive records inventory to verify that all documents are being properly managed.

Summary

In this chapter, we described the nature of records, why they are needed, and the problems that can arise if they are not managed correctly. We also noted the criteria that can be used for classifying records, which are used to assign varying levels of record storage and retention priorities. A records management system focuses on that last point, since it administers records throughout their life cycles, from creation to disposition.

In the next chapter, we delve into much more detail regarding record storage rules and storage systems.

Chapter 2
Record Storage Systems

Introduction

One of the most crucial aspects of a record management system is the method used to file records. The method chosen has an impact on the speed of filing and retrievals, as well as the rate of mis-files. In this chapter, we focus on several filing methods – alphabetic storage, subject storage, numeric storage, alphanumeric storage, and geographic storage.

Alphabetic Storage

The most common method for filing records is to arrange them in accordance with the letters of the alphabet. This approach does not require an index. Instead, users can go directly to the relevant records, which makes alphabetic storage a *direct access* method. This is quite a simple storage method, since only a knowledge of the alphabetical ordering of records is needed to access files.

While alphabetic storage might seem obvious, a set of rules must be constructed and followed religiously in order to ensure that records can be consistently and expeditiously filed and retrieved.

To properly store a record under an alphabetic storage system, one should engage in the following steps:

Step 1 – Indexing. The individual involved in the storage process must determine the *filing segment* used to index a record. A filing segment is the name under which a record is both stored and later requested by users. This filing segment is then used to place the record in alphabetical order. This initial step is critical, for the person must accurately determine the filing segment every time. Otherwise, an incorrect filing segment might be used, resulting in incorrect record storage that essentially results in the loss of a record, since it is not located where one might reasonably expect it to be. Examples of filing segments are:

- The name of a supplier, when storing a supplier invoice
- The name of an employee, when storing an employee file
- The number of a job, when storing a job record

When selecting a filing segment, the key issue is to use the one most likely to be used in the future when someone requests the record.

The designation of a filing segment is not the lowest unit of information used in alphabetic storage. Instead, each part of a filing segment is broken down further into *indexing units*. Indexing units are the words that comprise a filing segment. There may be a number of indexing units, which are labeled with a unit designation, such as:

- *Key unit*. The first unit in a filing segment, it is examined first when evaluating where to store a record.
- *Unit 2*. The next unit to be used after a key unit, when evaluating where to store a record.
- *Unit 3*. The second unit to be used after a key unit, when evaluating where to store a record.
- *Additional units*. There may be additional units added beyond Unit 3, depending on the number of words in a filing segment.

The order in which the units of a filing segment are considered for record storage is called the *indexing order*.

Step 2 – Coding. A file designation is applied to records as they go through the indexing process. This involves clearly identifying the filing segment by which a record will be stored. This coding step requires a physical action to designate a record.

For a physical record, the coding process involves the placement of diagonals (/) between each of the indexing units in a filing segment, and underlining the key unit. For example, the coding for Ulysses S. Grant would be:

Grant / Ulysses / S.

In the example, the indexing units are identified as follows:

Key unit	Grant
Unit 2	Ulysses
Unit 3	S.

The use of diagonals and underlining to identify indexing units is called *indexing rules*. It is not necessary to use diagonals and underlining as indexing rules; any other markings may also be considered indexing rules. The key point is to use these rules consistently, no matter how they are formulated.

Indexing rules are used to determine the correct alphabetic order for a group of filing segments. The essential process flow is as follows:

1. Compare the key units in the filing segments, and sort based on the differences in these indexing units.
2. If the key units are identical, compare the Unit 2 indexing units, and sort based on the difference in these indexing units.
3. Use the same approach for any additional indexing rules.

EXAMPLE

Inscription International manufactures and sells titanium pens. It sells through a large number of high-end retailers around the world. In the most recent month, the company enters into retailing agreements with several new stores, for which customer folders have been created. The names of these retailers are:

> Paper and Pen
> Papers International Ltd.
> Pago Pago Pen Company
> Paper Supplies Company

The coding for these names is as follows:

> <u>Paper</u> / and / Pen
> <u>Papers</u> / International / Ltd.
> <u>Pago</u> / Pago / Pen / Company
> <u>Paper</u> / Supplies / Company

The records can easily be sorted based on the key unit in each filing segment, with the exceptions of the two retailers whose names both begin with "Paper". For these two entities, the sort sequence is based on Unit 2, with "and" being sorted ahead of "Supplies". The file sort sequence for the four new retailers is:

> Pago Pago Pen Company
> Paper and Pen
> Paper Supplies Company
> Papers International Ltd.

Step 3 – Cross-referencing. In some cases, a physical record is likely to be called by two or more names. In these situations, a cross-reference must be created. A cross-reference presents a different name than the one used for the original record; it is used to state the location of the original record. With the careful use of cross-references, it is much more likely that a user can locate a record. Cross-references may not be necessary for electronic records, since database search tools can search entire documents.

A copy of a document may be stored in the cross-reference location, or a sheet containing the cross-reference can be prepared and inserted in the records at the relevant location.

> **Tip:** Limit the use of cross-referencing, since it takes extra time to document each cross-reference, and too many of them can clutter the files.

Personal Name Cross-Referencing

There are several situations in which a cross-reference may be needed for a personal name. They are:

- *Alternate names*. There may be situations in which a person does business under a different name. For example, a professional who has built up a reputation under her own name gets married. She adopts the name of her husband, but retains her original name for business purposes. A cross reference is needed to connect the two names.

EXAMPLE

Janice Dancik is a well-known tax partner at a prestigious national accounting firm. She marries Dennis Clinton, and decides to change her legal name to Janice Clinton, while retaining her maiden name for professional purposes. This presents a problem for the company's payroll staff, which uses a filing segment in which the key unit is Clinton. In case there is confusion about where to deliver her paychecks, a cross-reference is prepared that states her maiden name and the cross-reference, as follows:

<u>Clinton</u> / Janice

SEE Dancik

- *Hyphenation*. A person may marry and then add the other person's name on to his or her original name. To ensure that this modified name can still be found, prepare a cross-reference that states the person's original name.

EXAMPLE

Adrianne Underwood marries John Cahill, and uses hyphenation to change her name to Adrianne Underwood-Cahill. A person preparing Adrianne's personnel folder creates a filing segment in which the key unit is Underwood-Cahill. In case people are still searching for her maiden name, a cross-reference is prepared that has a filing segment in which the key unit is "Underwood" and Unit 2 is "Adrianne," as follows:

<u>Underwood</u> / Adrianne

SEE UnderwoodCahill

- *Naming confusion*. It may be difficult to determine a person's last name. The standard naming convention is to then assume that the last stated name is the person's actual last name. To guard against this not being the case, prepare a cross-reference that flips the names.

EXAMPLE

A person is preparing a file for a new customer, whose name is stated as Peyton Lindsay. Since both names could be considered first names, she prepares a filing segment in which the key unit is "Lindsay" and Unit 2 is "Peyton". In case the order of these names has been reversed, she also prepares a cross-reference that states:

Peyton / Lindsay

SEE Lindsay

- *Similar names.* Some names can be spelled multiple ways. If so, prepare a cross-reference for each possible name. For example, White can also be spelled Whyte, while Payne can be spelled Paine.

Business Name Cross-Referencing

There are several situations in which a cross-reference may be needed for a business name. They are:

- *Abbreviated names.* When a business is known by an abbreviated name or an acronym, prepare a cross-reference that spells out the full business name.

EXAMPLE

IBM is the abbreviation for International Business Machines. The cross-reference for the firm would be:

International / Business / Machines

SEE IBM

- *Changed names.* A company may change its name. If so, prepare a cross-reference that traces back to the original company name.

EXAMPLE

The board of directors of Hazardous Garbage Products decides that the company name is not helping its business, and so decides to change the name to Smiley Products. A customer of the new Smiley Products creates the following cross-reference:

Smiley / Products

See Hazardous Garbage Products

- *Compound names.* A firm name may include the surnames of several founders. If so, create a cross-reference for each of these names, so that someone can access the relevant record from any one name.

EXAMPLE

A payables clerk is preparing a supplier file for the company's law firm, which is Hickes, Dwight & Dunn. The two related cross-references that he creates are:

<u>Dwight</u> / Dunn / and / Hickes

SEE Hickes Dwight and Dunn

<u>Dunn</u> / Hickes / and / Dwight

SEE Hickes Dwight and Dunn

- *Foreign names.* When indexing the name of a foreign business, first convert it to the English version of the name and index it based on the English version. This presents the risk that someone could search for the name under its foreign spelling, so prepare a cross-reference for the foreign language version of the name.

EXAMPLE

A company sells training materials to Universidad Americana in Paraguay. The name translates into English as American University, so the filing segment is created based on that name. This results in the following cross-reference:

<u>Universidad</u> / Americana

SEE American University

- *Similar names.* There are cases in which a business name could be split apart or aggregated through common usage, with a result that differs from the actual company name. If so, prepare a cross-reference for each possible common usage variation on the business name.

EXAMPLE

Northeast Burgers is a company's name, but common usage could result in the name instead being recorded as North East Burgers. This results in the following cross-reference:

<u>North</u> / East / Burgers

SEE Northeast Burgers

- *Subsidiaries*. When a business is a subsidiary of a larger entity, the key unit is the name of the subsidiary. In addition, prepare a cross-reference back to the parent entity.

EXAMPLE

Suzanne LaCoste is a perfume distributor that is owned by the parent company, High Fashion Products. A retailer that buys from Suzanne LaCoste prepares the following cross-reference:

<u>High</u> / Fashion / Products

SEE Suzanne Lacoste

Step 4 – Sorting. When physical records are being used, the next step in an alphabetic storage system is to arrange the records in the sequence indicated in the preceding coding stage. We note a number of rules for sorting, segregated for personal and business names.

Personal Name Sorting

The key rules to remember when sorting personal names are as follows:

- *Personal names*. The last name (surname) is designated as the key unit, while the first name is the second unit, and the middle name is the third unit.
- *Identification of the last name*. Some names do not have a recognizable surname (most likely with foreign names). In these situations, assume that the last name written is the surname.
- *Nicknames and abbreviations*. Nicknames and abbreviations of names are sorted as written. For example, "Vicki" is sorted as written.
- *Precedence of initials*. When a name is presented as just an initial, the initial precedes an indexing unit that contains a complete name, on the theory that the initial is followed by nothing, and nothing always precedes all other letters.
- *Punctuation*. Punctuation is omitted for sorting purposes.

These rules are used in the following table, where we present a series of presorted personal names and then show how the sorting was accomplished by indexing unit. In each row, the underscored letter indicates the letter that triggered each sort.

Sample Sort for Personal Names

FILING SEGMENT	INDEXING ORDER		
Individual Name	Key Unit	Unit 2	Unit 3
Adam Babcock	Babcock	Adam	
Michael Babcock	Babcock	Michael	
Jeffrey A. Davis	Davis	Jeffrey	A
Jeffrey D. Davis	Davis	Jeffrey	D
Phillip Davis	Davis	Phillip	
Sarah Franklin	Franklin	Sarah	
Juliette Hewlett	Hewlett	Juliette	
Arlo Gastonbury	Gastonbury	Arlo	
Bruce F. Gastonbury	Gastonbury	Bruce	F
Bruce G. Gastonbury	Gastonbury	Bruce	G

Business Name Sorting

The key issues to remember when sorting business names are as follows:

- *Business names.* Business names are sorted as written, so there is no presumption that a "last name" within a business name is indexed first. Instead, the first word in the name is assumed to be the key unit.
- *Business names containing personal names.* If there is a personal name within a business name (such as "Adam's Best Burgers"), the first word in the name is still assumed to be the key unit.
- *Acronyms.* An acronym is assigned a single indexing unit. Thus, the radio station WBEZ is treated as a single indexing unit, as would IBM.
- *Punctuation.* Punctuation is omitted for sorting purposes. For example, "Charley's Burgers" is sorted as though it were spelled "Charleys Burgers". Similarly, "D'Angelo" is sorted as though it were spelled "DAngelo". As another example, "Inter-Mountain Express" is sorted as though it were spelled "InterMountain Express."
- *Single letters.* Single letters in a business name are assigned a separate indexing unit. For example, "A B C Realty" would have "A" as its key unit and "B" as its Unit 2, while "ABC Realty" would have "ABC" as its key unit and "Realty" as its Unit 2.
- *Symbols.* When a symbol appears in a business name, it is spelled out. For example, "$" is sorted as though it were spelled as "Dollar" and "&" is treated as "and". Further, "@" is treated as "at" while "%" is treated as "percent".
- *The.* When the word "The" is used as the first word of a business name, it is considered to be the last indexing unit. For example, "The Wine Place" is treated as "Wine Place, The."

These rules are used in the following table, where we present a series of presorted business names and then show how the sorting was accomplished by indexing unit. In each row, the underscored letter indicates the letter that triggered each sort.

Sample Sorting of Business Names

FILING SEGMENT	INDEXING ORDER		
Business Name	Key Unit	Unit 2	Unit 3
A.B. Smith & Sons	A	B	Smith
Bentley by Design	Bentley	by	Design
Bentley Motor Sales	Bentley	Motor	Sales
Charley's Burgers	Charleys	Burgers	
Chisholm Medical Clinic	Chisholm	Medical	Clinic
Deadly Force Pest Control	Deadly	Force	Pest
Deadly Skid Insurance Co.	Deadly	Skid	Insurance
Iron Castings Company	Iron	Castings	Company
Ironwood Furniture Products	Ironwood	Furniture	Products
Irony Business Writing	Irony	Business	Writing
The Last $	Last	Dollar	The

Additional Alphabetic Storage Rules – Personal Names

There are several additional rules that apply to the sorting of personal names, which are:

- *Title before a name*. When a title appears before a name, classify it as the last indexing unit. For example, "Professor" or "Sir" would be listed last.
- *Seniority suffix*. When a seniority suffix appears, classify it as the last indexing unit. For example, "Jr." or "Sr." would be listed last.
- *Professional suffix*. When a professional designation appears as a suffix, classify it as the last indexing unit. For example, "CPA" would be listed last.
- *Numeric priority*. A numeric suffix, such as "III" is classified before an alphabetic suffix, such as "PhD".
- *Title and suffix*. If a name contains both a title and a suffix, the title is assigned the last indexing unit.
- *Religious titles*. If a name contains a religious title and only one additional name, such as "Sister Mary," assign indexing units as the name is written.

These rules are used in the following table, where we present a series of presorted personal names and then show how the sorting was accomplished by indexing unit. In each row, the underscored letter indicates the letter that triggered each sort.

Sample Sort for Personal Names

FILING SEGMENT	INDEXING ORDER			
Individual Name	Key Unit	Unit 2	Unit 3	Unit 4
Dr. Amos Breeze	Breeze	Amos	Dr	
Mr. Amos Breeze PhD	Breeze	Amos	PhD	Mr
Cardinal John Carroll	Carroll	John	Cardinal	
Steven L. Dugan III	Dugan	Steven	L	III
Steven L. Dugan Jr.	Dugan	Steven	L	Jr
Steven L. Dugan Sr.	Dugan	Steven	L	Sr
Ms. Ellen Heathrow, CPA	Heathrow	Ellen	CPA	Ms
Miss Ellen Heathrow	Heathrow	Ellen	Miss	
Mrs. Ellen Heathrow	Heathrow	Ellen	Mrs	
Sister Doreen	Sister	Doreen		

Additional Alphabetic Storage Rules – Business Names

There are several additional rules that apply to the sorting of business names, which are:

- *Title in name.* A title in a business name is indexed as it is written. Various sorts using this rule are noted in the following sample.

Sample Sort for Business Names

FILING SEGMENT	INDEXING ORDER		
Business Name	Key Unit	Unit 2	Unit 3
Captain Rick's Flight Service	Captain	Ricks	Flight
Granny's Popovers	Grannys	Popovers	
High Flyin' Mike's	High	Flyin	Mikes
Mom and Pop's Ice Cream	Mom	and	Pops
Surgeon Paul's Medicines	Surgeon	Pauls	Medicines

- *Numbers spelled out.* When a business spells out a number within its name, the spelled-out number is used for sorting purposes. Examples are "Three Little Pigs Construction" and Two Rivers Condominiums".
- *Numbers as digits.* When numbers appear in a business name as digits, they are sorted before numbers that have been spelled out. Thus, "Number 1 Bakery" appears before "Number One Bakery". Also, numbers are sorted in ascending order, so that "21 Jump Street" appears before "22 Jump Street".
- *Additional numeric designators.* When a number ends in *nd*, *rd*, or *st*, ignore these extra letters and only sort based on the numbers. For example, "1st," "2nd," and "3rd" are treated as 1, 2, and 3.

- *Hyphen separation.* When hyphens are used to separate multiple numbers, remove the hyphens. Thus, "1-2-3 Delivery Service" becomes "123 Delivery Service". Similarly, when names are hyphenated with a number, remove the hyphen. For example, "A-1 Lawn Mowing" becomes "A1 Lawn Mowing".

These rules are used in the following table, where we present a series of presorted business names and then show how the sorting was accomplished by indexing unit. In each row, the underscored letter indicates the letter that triggered each sort.

Sample Sort for Business Names

FILING SEGMENT	INDEXING ORDER		
Business Name	Key Unit	Unit 2	Unit 3
1-2-3 Home Repair	123	Home	Repair
2-3-5 Prime Number Math Tutoring	235	Prime	Number
3rd Street Tailors	3	Street	Tailors
One Way Clothiers	One	Way	Clothiers
Two Wing Aerobatics	Two	Wing	Aerobatics

What about situations in which a business letter needs to be indexed? In these situations, the indexing is based on the following rules:

- Assign the key unit to the business name on the letterhead.
- When there is no relationship between the business name on the letterhead and the name of the writer, assign the key unit to the writer's name.
- When the company name and the writer's name are of equal importance, assign the key unit to the company name.

Miscellaneous Alphabetic Storage Rules

There are a few additional rules related to the sorting treatment of identical names and government names, which we address in the following sub-sections.

Identical Names

When sorting alphabetic names, a common problem is what to do when names are identical. This is an easy chore in an electronic records management system, since the user can just peruse other information pertaining to a name (such as a phone number or address) that can further refine the search. The situation is not quite so simple for a physical document, where the additional information is not so readily accessible. Instead, the additional search criterion is the address. For sorting purposes, the name is assigned the higher indexing units, after which additional indexing units are assigned in this order:

1. *City.* This is the official name of the city, with no abbreviations. Thus, "West Roxbury" is used, rather than "W. Roxbury".
2. *State or province.* The state or province name is spelled in full. Thus, "North Carolina" is used, rather than "NC".
3. *Street name.* This includes the full spelling of "Boulevard," "Street" or any other street designator, rather than their contractions.
4. *Building numbers.* These numbers are sorted in ascending numerical order. For example, "3 Smith Lane" will sort ahead of "415 Smith Lane".

These rules are used in the following table, where we present a series of presorted names and then show how the sorting was accomplished by indexing unit. In each row, the underscored letter indicates the letter that triggered each sort.

Sample Sort for Identical Names

FILING SEGMENT	INDEXING ORDER					
Business Name	Key Unit	Unit 2	Unit 3	Unit 4	Unit 5	Unit 6
Easy-Car-Care 158 3rd St. Denver, Colorado	EasyCarCare	Denver	Colorado	3	Street	158
Easy-Car-Care 456 Baseline Rd. Denver, Colorado	EasyCarCare	Denver	Colorado	Baseline	Road	456
Easy-Car-Care 100 Baseline St. Denver, Colorado	EasyCarCare	Denver	Colorado	Baseline	Street	100
Easy-Car-Care 12000 Dry Creek Rd. Denver, Colorado	EasyCarCare	Denver	Colorado	Dry Creek	Road	12000
Easy-Car-Care 14210 Dry Creek Rd. Denver, Colorado	EasyCarCare	Denver	Colorado	Dry Creek	Road	14210

Government Names

A business may deal with a large number of government entities, including the city, county, state, and country governments within which it maintains facilities and personnel. Each of the records related to these entities must be properly indexed. The following sequence is used to assign indexing units to government names:

1. *Government name.* Always assign the name of the government to the key unit. For example, the key unit for the City of Boston Water Department is "Boston", while the key unit for the Arapahoe County Metropolitan Wastewater Division is "Arapahoe".
2. *Distinctive name.* Assign to the second indexing unit the most distinctive part of the government entity's name. If a departmental designation is part of the name, this can precede what would otherwise be the second indexing unit.

This would be "Water" for our first example and "Metropolitan" for the second example.

These rules are used in the following table, where we present a series of presorted names and then show how the sorting was accomplished by indexing unit. In each row, the underscored letter indicates the letter that triggered each sort.

Sample Sort for City Government Names

FILING SEGMENT	INDEXING ORDER				
Government Name	Key Unit	Unit 2	Unit 3	Unit 4	Unit 5
Atlanta City Detention Center	Atlanta	City	Detention	Center	
Atlanta City Hall	Atlanta	City	Hall		
Atlanta Municipal Court	Atlanta	Municipal	Court		
Atlanta Parks & Recreation	Atlanta	Parks	and	Recreation	
Atlanta Department of Watershed Management	Atlanta	Watershed	Management	Department	of

The same rules apply to state governments, as noted in the following table.

Sample Sort for State Government Names

FILING SEGMENT	INDEXING ORDER				
Government Name	Key Unit	Unit 2	Unit 3	Unit 4	Unit 5
Georgia Division of Aging Services	Georgia	Aging	Services	Division	of
Georgia Department of Audits & Accounts	Georgia	Audits	and	Accounts	Department
Georgia Civil War Commission	Georgia	Civil	War	Commission	
Georgia Consumer Protection Unit	Georgia	Consumer	Protection	Unit	
Georgia Commission of Equal Opportunity	Georgia	Equal	Opportunity	Commission	of

The same rules apply to the federal government, as noted in the following table. The name of the country is assigned the key unit, after which the most distinctive part of the department name is assigned the second indexing unit. The words "of" and "of the" are not included in any indexing units at the federal government level.

Sample Sort for Federal Government Names

FILING SEGMENT	INDEXING ORDER		
Government Entity Name	Key Unit	Unit 2	Unit 3
Architect of the Capitol	United States Government	Architect	Capitol
Congressional Budget Office	United States Government	Congressional	Budget
Defense Contract Audit Agency	United States Government	Defense	Contract
Office of Economic Adjustment	United States Government	Economic	Adjustment
White House Transportation Agency	United States Government	White	House

Problems with Alphabetic Storage

Though alphabetic storage is a dominant storage system, it does suffer from a few problems. In particular, it is quite possible that records will not be filed correctly if users are not thoroughly conversant in the filing rules being used. Also, once a record has been mis-filed, it is extremely difficult to locate it again. Further, it can be easy to mix records when the correspondent names are quite similar. Thus, a record for A.B. Smith could easily be stored in a folder for A.C. Smith.

For these reasons, it is critical to have a well-trained and diligent group of employees. Whenever there is employee turnover, this presents the risk that the incoming person does not have a sufficiently high skill level with the storage system, and so will cause filing problems that may not be detected for some time.

Subject Storage

Though the alphabetic storage system described in the preceding sections is the predominant method in use, this type of records management is usually positioned underneath a subject (by topic) sort. For example, an accounting department will segregate its supplier invoices and customer invoices into separate accounts payable and accounts receivable topics, and then set up an alphabetic storage system underneath these separate topics. As additional examples, a company may separately store records under all of the following topics:

Customer orders	Purchase orders
Employee records	Resumes received
Fixed asset records	Shipments
Inventory records	Supplier contracts

There are times when an organization deals with a broad range of topics that must be stored and retrieved. For example, it may store the following:

Audio recordings	Reports
Clippings	Research data
E-mails	Video recordings

When there is such a broad array of storage possibilities, it can make more sense to adopt a record storage system that focuses on the subject, rather than an alphabetic listing. In a larger organization, it may be mandatory to have a certain amount of subject storage.

However, a subject storage system can present some difficulties. In particular, the number of topics may increase or be subdivided over time; this can result in overlaps where records could be tied to several different topics, or must be reassigned when a new topic is created. Also, as the number of topics increases, users may not remember them all, which leads to frustration with record searches. And finally, the addition of topics to the approved list can be a bureaucratic (and therefore annoying) process in which several departments may have different reasons for proposing alternative topics. To alleviate these concerns, adopt the following practices when creating a subject storage system:

- *Centralize topic-making.* One person should have final responsibility for the creation of new topics. Otherwise, if anyone is allowed to create a topic, the system will soon contain a number of conflicting topics.
- *Simplify topics.* Create topics that clearly state the topic, without being so arcane that users are confused. In particular, ensure that each topic selected cannot be misinterpreted.

One way to set up a records storage system by subject is to sort the topics in alphabetical order. This approach works well when there are not too many records to store, as would be the case with a small business. The following table shows such a filing system.

Sample Subject Storage System in Alphabetical Order

Letter	Subject Tabs
A	Autos
B	Banking
	Budget and Plans
C	Cell phones
	Customer Service
E	Employee Hire Dates
F	Fixed Asset Listings
G	Government Regulations
H	Hazardous Waste Reports
I	Inventory Summaries
J	Job Applications
M	Maintenance Records
O	Office Supplies
P	Payroll Information
Q	Quarterly Financial Statements
S	Sales Summaries
T	Tax Filings
	Time Cards and Time Sheets
V	Vacation Schedule
W	W-2 Forms

A different approach is to create a system in which records are filed under a topic and subtopic system. Under this approach, topics are still sorted in alphabetical order, but the emphasis is entirely on topics. For this reason, the main topic is printed on each folder tab, with the sub-topic listed below it. Also, a general topic folder is included at the end of a set of folders under a topic, which is used to accumulate all records that are not assigned to an individual folder. This general topic folder plays the same role as a general folder in an alphabetic record management system. The following exhibit shows such a filing system.

Sample Topic and Sub-Topic Storage System

Topic	Topic and Sub-Topic
Banking	Banking Credit Card Processing
	Banking Lockbox Agreements
	Banking Procurement Cards
	Banking General Folder
Personnel	Personnel Job Applications
	Personnel Union Agreements
	Personnel W-2 Forms
	Personnel General Folder

A good way to differentiate the tabs in a topic and sub-topic storage system is to assign a specific color to each topic and its associated sub-topics. For example, the banking topic in the preceding example and the four sub-topics associated with it could have red tabs. If one of these folders were to be mis-filed, the associated color would immediately stand out in the filing system.

It is not possible to purchase a pre-configured set of labels for this type of system (as is the case for an alphabetic system), since labels must be custom-created for topics and sub-topics. When creating these labels, use the same font for all labels. If there is a mix of fonts, labels are harder to read, which interferes with the filing and retrieval of records.

Any type of subject records system requires an index. A user first accesses the index to see if a topic exists and where the applicable folder is located, and then goes to the storage system to access the folder. Since this is a two-step process, it is called an *indirect access* method. An index is usually created and maintained on a computer. The primary indexing format to use is an alphabetic listing of all topics and sub-topics. Consider keeping a recent copy of the index in the records storage area, where it is easily accessible to users. Whenever the index changes, be sure to replace the printed copy in the records storage area with the newest version. A sample index with selected topics follows.

Sample Index for Selected Topics

Fixed Assets	Inventories
Buildings	Finished goods
Computer Equipment	Merchandise
Computer Software	Raw Materials
Furniture & Fixtures	Work-in-Process
Machinery	**Joint Ventures**
Vehicles	Contractual Arrangements
Goodwill	Financial Statements
Goodwill Calculations	Funding
Goodwill Impairment Testing	Termination Notices

A potential problem with a subject records management system is that documents may need to be perused in detail to ensure that the correct topic and sub-topic are selected. In addition, the most appropriate topic may not yet exist in the records storage system, which may call for additional discussion to determine whether an additional topic or sub-topic should be created. This can slow down the filing process.

Numeric Storage

A numeric storage system is one that arranges records based on numbers. For example, businesses are assigned tax identification numbers, while citizens are assigned social security numbers – both being used as unique identifiers.

A numeric records management system is used in environments that have either of the following two characteristics:

- There is a strong need to keep records confidential by not assigning a name to them
- Large numbers of records are routinely filed and retrieved

Under this system, a unique number is assigned to each record, and that number becomes the basis upon which the record is filed. Thus, in a series of records to which numbers have been assigned, the record assigned "10" will be filed ahead of another record to which "50" has been assigned, irrespective of the contents of the records. If someone were to see the outside of one of these folders, they would have no idea of its contents, since the assigned number on the folder provides no usable information.

A numeric records management system is considered an indirect access system, since one must first review an index to determine the number associated with a record, and use that number to access the record.

The most common number assignment system is consecutive numbering, where the numbering begins with a lower number, and ascends from there. When this approach is translated into a physical filing system, the tab layout could appear as noted in the following example, where the tab on a guide is the beginning number for a sequence of files, with the numbered individual files appearing thereafter. The guides represent markers that filers can use to zero in on files. We discuss guides in the next chapter.

Sample Numeric Storage System

Guide	Folder
100	
	101 – Wilson Lawn Care Services
	102 – Monk Bakery and Deli
	103 – Puma Exotic Meat Butchers
	104 – Aardvark Pet Care International
	105 – Quigley's Environmental Containment Systems
	106 – Smith Personnel Folder
	107 – Expense Reports (A-C)
	108 – Resumes Received (R-T)
	109 – Quarterly Financial Statements
110	

An alternative to the presentation in the preceding exhibit is to only include numbers on the folder tabs, which greatly increases the level of confidentiality. Someone would have to open a folder in order to determine its contents.

When a numeric records management system is used, it is still quite possible that a set of general folders will be needed for the storage of miscellaneous records related to low-volume correspondents. When this is the case, it will be necessary to maintain a set of general folders that are filed in alphabetic sequence. These general folders are usually positioned in front of the numerically-ordered folders. If the record volume increases for a correspondent, records may be removed from a general folder and shifted into a separate, numerically-filed folder.

When the numbers for a numeric records management system are being manually assigned to records, the person authorized to issue the numbers must maintain an *accession log*. This is a logbook in which the individual maintains a serial listing of every number issued for a record, along with the record name and the date on which the number was issued. Without this log, a person could easily assign a number to several different records. This log is most efficiently maintained as a computer database.

In order to locate records in this type of system, an alphabetic index must be constructed that associates each assigned number to the name of the underlying record. Users then search the names in the index to find out where records are located within the filing system. This index should almost always be a computer file, since it may be quite large and will be updated continuously. A sample alphabetic index follows.

Sample Alphabetic Index

Name / Subject	File Number
A1 Plumbing Services	1063
Arlo's Heating and Ventilation Repair Shop	1079
Bingo and Casino Supply Company	1001
Casino Gaming Rentals	1042
Chartered Furniture International	1099
Dresden Chinaware	1214
Elderly Care Hostels	1083
Fallow Crops Feed and Fertilizer	1405
Gregorian Chants Party Singers	1311
Hi-Value Entertainment Services	1209

Before deciding to use a numeric filing system, consider a potential problem with this method, and how it might impact a filing operation. The most recent records are all assigned the highest numbers, so these records are filed together at the physical end of the filing system (such as the last filing cabinet). The most recent records tend to experience the most filing and retrieval activity, so it is possible that there will be a high degree of staff congestion where these records are located.

Alphanumeric Storage

An alphanumeric records management system combines subject (sorted alphabetically) and numeric filing systems. Typically, this means that a subject is initially used, followed by one or more numeric designations. For example, a company might store its sales orders by state, listing the sales orders numerically within each state. Thus, a record coding of MN-100752 would indicate sales order number 100752, which originated within the state of Minnesota. Another example appears in the following exhibit, which shows an alphanumeric system for the designation of records in a company's procedures manual.

Sample Alphanumeric Coding for a Procedures Manual

Alphanumeric Coding	Topic and Sub-Topic
ACCT-AP-05	Accounting Department | Accounts Payable | Invoice Approvals
ACCT-AP-10	Accounting Department | Accounts Payable | Invoice Data Entry
ACCT-AP-15	Accounting Department | Accounts Payable | Supplier Payments
ACCT-AR-05	Accounting Department | Accounts Receivable | Credit Memo Processing
ACCT-AR-10	Accounting Department | Accounts Receivable | Debit Memo Processing
ACCT-AR-15	Accounting Department | Accounts Receivable | Payment Processing
ACCT-GL-05	Accounting Department | General Ledger | Closing the Books
ACCT-GL-10	Accounting Department | General Ledger | One-Time Entries
ACCT-GL-15	Accounting Department | General Ledger | Recurring Entries

Alphanumeric systems can work quite well, but require additional staff training to fully understand how they function. Without a high level of staff knowledge, this type of system can experience an unusually high level of record mis-files.

Geographic Storage

Some records are most easily accessed based on the location to which they refer. For example, a record may relate to a company location, city, state, region, country, or continent. This is a common situation in businesses that deal with land rights, such as oil exploration or ranching firms, as well as governments that routinely deal with property rights. It is especially common in multi-national corporations that may operate in dozens of countries. In these situations, a geographic storage system is used. A sample arrangement appears in the following exhibit, where a facility management department for a large multi-national corporation needs to track facility records across several continents. Accordingly, the records storage system is initially tabbed by continent, then country, and then city.

Sample Geographic Storage System

Guide	Special Guide	Folder
North America		
	Canada	
		Calgary
		Montreal
		Vancouver
	Mexico	
		Guadalajara
		Mexico City
		Monterrey
	United States	
		Los Angeles
		Miami
		New York

The label on each folder tab may include both the guide and special guide information, which makes it more difficult to mis-file the folder. For example, the tab for the Montreal folder in the preceding exhibit could be printed as follows:

N.A.	Canada
	Montreal

In this tab, the "N.A." designation indicates that the folder belongs in the North America geographic region. The additional listings of Canada and then Montreal further refine the region.

The information in the preceding exhibit was essentially an alphabetic filing system, since the geographic locations were sorted in alphabetical order. This information could also be converted to a numeric filing system, where assigned numbers are swapped for each of the geographic locations. For example, if North America had been assigned #01 as a filing code, Canada had a #250 code, and Calgary had a #1045 code, then the Calgary location in the preceding exhibit would have been coded as 01-250-1045.

As another example of a geographic filing system, a hospital is keeping track of multiple projects in one of its campus buildings, as presented in the following exhibit. The building name is used as the primary guide, after which project numbers are assigned to each construction project currently under way within that building, based on the floor on which they are situated.

Sample Construction Project Coding

Building	Floor	Project
Ames Building	2	01
		04
		05
	4	17

The key improvement offered by a geographic storage system is that records pertaining to a specific location are grouped together. This is quite useful when someone routinely needs to access blocks of records pertaining to the same location. For example, a facilities manager learns that a city has just upgraded its building codes pertaining to air conditioning. He can use this type of system to quickly access all company-owned buildings within the city limits, to see which facilities might fail the new requirements.

The main downside to this system is that a user must know the geographic location in order to access a record. Thus, this approach is more likely to work well in an environment where users are highly knowledgeable, or where an index is also compiled that lists the location code for each record. Another concern is that geographic names in English are not necessarily the same in the local language, so cross-referencing may be needed to direct users from the local name to where records are filed under the English name.

Summary

An alphabetic filing system is likely to be the default system adopted in most situations, since it is highly intuitive. We have also noted several other filing systems, which will be applicable under more specialized circumstances. There is a good chance that an organization may employ a mix of these systems, depending on its needs.

All of these systems require a good knowledge of filing rules to avoid mis-filings, so the filing staff should be well-trained before being allowed anywhere near the record storage system.

Chapter 3
Elements of a Records Management System

Introduction

There are many issues to consider when operating a records management system, in addition to what was addressed in the last chapter. In this chapter, we cover record storage equipment and supplies, record preparation, filing, requisitions and returns, retention schedules, and record destruction. In addition, we have compiled a number of best practices related to records management that can enhance the efficiency and effectiveness of the system.

Record Storage Equipment

There are several types of storage equipment used for physical records. They are as follows:

- *Lateral file cabinets*. This is a cabinet in which the width of the unit exceeds its depth. The narrower depth of this arrangement makes these cabinets ideal for storing records in narrower aisles. Hanging folders (as described in the next section) are typically used to store records within each drawer of the cabinet. The sort order can begin at either end, or from front to back. A two-drawer configuration is most convenient for use next to a desk, while four and five-drawer configurations are used for general storage. It requires about one foot of aisle space to pull out a drawer.
- *Vertical file cabinets*. This is a cabinet in which the depth of the unit exceeds its width. Hanging folders are normally used to store records within each drawer of the cabinet. The sort order for the hanging folders is from front to back. A two-drawer configuration is most convenient for use next to a desk, while four and five-drawer configurations are used for general storage. The standard cabinet width is designed to hold letter-size paper, while a wider version is available for legal-size paper. It requires about two feet of aisle space to pull out a drawer.
- *Mobile shelving*. This is a set of shelves that move on tracks in a carousel system, so that a person can access multiple drawers without moving. It is the most expensive type of record storage equipment, but also maximizes the use of available storage space.
- *Shelf files*. This is an open shelf, where records are accessed from the side. It is the least expensive type of record storage equipment. It also requires minimal aisle space, since there is no drawer to pull out. It works well in situations where a large number of files must be frequently retrieved, such as a medical

office. However, this is the least secure storage option, since there is no drawer that can be locked to prevent unauthorized access to records.

The type of storage equipment used will depend on the circumstances. When records are confidential, locking cabinets are the best choice. When there is less aisle space available in which to pull out drawers, lateral file cabinets are a good choice. When there is very little storage space available, all options except for vertical file cabinets should be considered. When there is a hefty budget for storage equipment, consider using mobile shelving, since it is the easiest to access and makes the best use of the cubic volume available.

In general, the selection of storage equipment should focus on making the task of accessing records as easy as possible. Most other considerations are secondary to this item.

Record storage is a bad area in which to save money by purchasing inferior or light-duty equipment. Such equipment has a strong tendency to stick, so that drawers do not pull out smoothly (if at all), which incrementally increases the work load of anyone attempting to access records. Instead, this is a good area in which to spend more to obtain high-quality, robust equipment.

Record Storage Supplies

A number of supplies can be used in the storage of physical records. In the following sub-sections, we briefly describe each one.

Guides and Special Guides

A *guide* is a rigid cardboard or plastic divider that is used to signal the start of a new section within a group of records. The use of a reasonable number of guides at regular intervals within a filing system makes it easier for people to locate records. The simplest set of guides can be purchased that contains a separate guide for each letter of the alphabet, as well as for the numbers one through nine. More extensive sets of guides can be purchased that incorporate subsets of the alphabet (such as a separate guide for "Mc"). Blank guides can also be purchased, so that company-specific guides can be created. Guide tabs must extend up or to the side, so that they can be easily seen.

A *special guide* is the same as a guide, which indicates sub-levels of information within a record storage location. In the following exhibit, we show guides that signal the start of a new alphabetic section of a record storage system, followed by subdivisions that are indicated by special guides, and within which folders are located. The use of special guides makes it easier for employees to locate the relevant sections of record storage.

Sample Alphabetic Storage System

Guide	Special Guide	Folder
A		
	Alpharetta	
		Alpharetta Welding Supply
		American Gas Providers
		American Interstate Transport Services
	Animal	
		Animal Feedstock Services
		Applewood Farmers' Cooperative
		Atwood Brothers Drone Spraying, Inc.
B		
	Black	
		Black and Tan Scottish Supplies
		Bridle Horse Trainers, International
		Browne & Belvidere Roofing
	Borrow	
		Borrow More Financial Services
		Byway Farm Equipment Rentals

Tabs

A tab is a projection that rises above the edge of a folder or guide, and which contains indexing information.

Folders

A folder is a cardboard container that holds the records in a file. The best folders contain *score marks*, which are indented lines along the bottom edge that can be folded along to expand the storage capacity of the folder. A folder usually contains a tab, on which is pasted the filing segment for the relevant record. Several folder variations are:

- *Top tab*. A top tab folder has a tab extending out of the top of the folder. It is intended for storage in a filing cabinet, where access is from the top.
- *End tab*. An end tab folder has a tab extending from the side of the folder. It is intended for shelf storage, where access is from the side.

There are a number of tab styles that can be applied to both top tab and end tab configurations. A straight cut tab extends across the entire top or side of a folder. A one-third cut means that the tab extends across one-third of the top or side. Similarly, a one-fifth cut means that the tab extends across one-fifth of the top or side. Tabs are commonly placed in a staggered arrangement, starting on the left and progressing to the right. For example, in a one-third cut folder, the first tab position is reserved for the guides, the second tab position is reserved for the special guides, and the third tab position is reserved for the folders. This tab placement is illustrated in the following example, where we employ a compressed version of the preceding exhibit, with an extra row inserted to indicate tab positions.

Sample Alphabetic Storage Tab Positions

Guide	Special Guide	Folder
1st Tab	**2nd Tab**	**3rd Tab**
A		
	Alpharetta	
		Alpharetta Welding Supply
B		
	Black	
		Black and Tan Scottish Supplies

Folders may be employed in several ways. A *general folder* contains records that involve small volumes, where there is no need for a specially-designated folder. For example, there is a "C" folder at the end of the "C" section of folders that holds all miscellaneous records. Records are arranged within this folder alphabetically by correspondent name. An *individual folder* is used to store only the records for a specific correspondent; it is typically employed when there is a sufficient volume of records to warrant a separate folder. Records are arranged within this folder by date, with the most recently-dated records first.

The preceding two types of folders were the same physical version of a folder, but used for different purposes. The following are specialized folders that are designed for more specific uses:

- *Bellows folder.* A bellows folder is a free-standing folder that contains a number of built-in dividers. It is used to store records when the total volume of records is quite small. For example, the bookkeeper of a small company might find that a bellows folder is sufficient for storing all unpaid accounts payable.
- *Hanging folder.* A hanging folder contains hooks on each side that are suspended from the rails in a file drawer. Plastic tabs are then added to the upper edge of these folders. General and individual folders are placed within a hanging folder. These folders are highly useful for maintaining an orderly filing system.

Additional Supplies

There are several other supplies that can be of use in a records management system. The *follower block* is a metal plate at the back of a file drawer that can be adjusted to reduce the effective length of the drawer. This adjustment is used to keep folders upright in the front of the drawer. Otherwise, the folders will sag, which can damage them and also makes it more difficult to access folders. A follower block is not needed when hanging folders are used, since these folders are suspended from side rails and so will not slide down.

An *OUT indicator* is a sheet or folder that indicates the location of records that have been removed from storage. This indicator contains space to write in the name of the person who removed the records, the date of the removal, and the due date for its return. There may also be room for a notation regarding the contents of the removed records. The indicator is inserted into the files when records are removed, and is pulled out when the records are returned. To make the indicator easy to find, it may have a bright color, and includes a large tab with the word "OUT" printed on it. Not only is an OUT indicator useful for keeping track of records, it also reduces the work required to find the location in which to re-insert records.

Record Preparation and Filing

There are several steps to take when preparing physical records for storage, so that they are not damaged and can be easily accessed. The steps can be divided into record preparation and record filing, as follows:

Record Preparation

- *Combine documents*. Remove all paper clips being used to fasten documents together. Instead, staple these documents in the upper right corner. The use of this corner means that other records being inserted into a folder will not be accidentally inserted between stapled pages.
- *Repair documents*. Use tape to cover over any document tears. Otherwise, there is a risk that the records will be more extensively torn when filed or removed from folders.

Record Filing

1. *Identify folder*. See if there is an individual folder into which the record can be filed. If not, move to the general folder for the applicable letter range.
2. *Raise folder*. Raise the applicable folder, to ensure that the record is placed in that folder, rather than an adjacent folder.
3. *Position record*. File each record in a folder with its top to the left. By doing so, stapled sets of records have the staple in the top, so that no other records can be inadvertently inserted between them. Also, the most recent record is positioned in the front of the folder.
4. *Replace in order*. When replacing a record in a folder, insert it in the correct chronological sequence, to avoid record jumbling.

Physical Record Requisition and Return

A key component of a records management system is having a well thought-out process in place for requisitioning records from storage, and then returning them to storage. Without such a process, employees will spend far too much time tracking down missing records.

We begin with the record requisition. This is a form in which is itemized the name of the person borrowing the record and that person's contact information, as well as the date by which the record is supposed to be returned. A sample form appears in the following exhibit. One copy of this form is inserted into the folder from which the record was removed, to indicate who has the record. The requestor retains a copy of the form, as a reminder of when to return the record. The information on the form may also be recorded in a charge-out log by the records management staff; this log is used to track down records that have not yet been returned. A sample charge-out log appears in a following exhibit. Once a record is returned, the withdrawal is checked off in the charge-out log, and the requisition form is removed from the folder.

Sample Requisition Form

RECORDS REQUISITION FORM	
Record Name: Caterpillar Inc.	
Date Withdrawn: May 16, 20X2	Return by Date: May 20, 20X2
Requester Name: Eleanor Ridley	Requester E-mail: e.ridley@....
Requester Department: Accounts Payable	Requester Phone Extension: x314

If a record has been stamped confidential or essential, this places a restriction on the ability of the records management staff to release it from storage. If a person requests such a document, they should obtain additional approval from a corporate officer before it will be released. It may only be allowable to inspect certain records in a secure room, from which the records cannot be removed. In this situation, the name of the person inspecting the record will be logged, in case there is ever a question about who accessed the record.

> **Tip:** Minimize the period during which employees are allowed to retain records outside of storage. The longer the retention period, the more difficult it is to retrieve the records.

Sample Charge-Out Log

Record Name	Record Date	Requester Name	Contact Info	Date Withdrawn	Due Date	Date Returned
Alpha Micro	Feb. 14	L. Billups	x312	Apr. 4	Apr. 8	Apr. 5
Big Brother Industries	Jan. 11	R. Josephson	x104	Apr. 4	Apr. 8	Apr. 7
Caterpillar Inc.	Feb. 27	J. Woodson	x704	Apr. 7	Apr. 11	
Diamond Research	Mar. 27	T. Daniels	x441	Apr. 7	Apr. 11	Apr. 9
Everyman Engineering	Mar. 10	S. Crew	x222	Apr. 7	Apr. 11	

Record Transfers

Records may be periodically transferred from active to inactive storage. This transfer typically occurs at a set time each year. When this happens, folders are shifted into long-term storage boxes, and new folders are prepared for the current period. There is no need for the inclusion of guides in the long-term storage boxes, since there is little expectation that they will be needed to assist users.

When records are shifted to a storage box, the box is clearly labeled with the contents. It can make sense to label both ends of the box with the same information; this can be helpful when boxes are incorrectly stacked in the inactive storage area, so that an unlabeled side would otherwise face outward.

In a high-volume environment in which many records are being transferred, it can make sense to also use a records transmittal and receipt form. This form is used to document the movement of records from a transferring department to inactive storage. This document states which records are being moved, and requires the signatures of the releasing and accepting managers.

Once records have been stored in inactive storage, the record center staff enters the location and box contents information into an inactive records index. This index may include several other items of information, such as the retention period, the disposition date, and the name of the originating department. The index is especially useful for tracking down box locations for record requests, as well as for flagging which records are due for final disposition.

The procedures followed for the removal and return of inactive records are the same as those noted earlier for active records. A records requisition form is required when anyone wants to access a record, and these forms are logged into a charge-out log. The log is regularly monitored to ensure that records are returned by users. While records are being used by the requestors, an OUT indicator replaces the record in the inactive files, indicating that a record is currently missing.

The Records Retention Schedule

With the exception of essential records, most records can be destroyed after a certain period of time has passed. This is of some importance when the records take up a substantial amount of storage space, since the organization is paying for this space. In addition, the firm is paying for an excessive amount of record storage equipment, and a certain amount of staff time to keep track of and periodically move the records. Consequently, a records retention schedule should be constructed that itemizes how long each type of record should be kept.

When discussing record retention criteria earlier, we noted that there are four general classifications into which records can be placed, which are nonessential information, useful records, important records, and essential records. In a general sense, we can assign approximate retention periods based on these classifications, which are:

- *Nonessential information*. If a record is not worth keeping, it can be disposed of at once. Examples are voice mails and e-mails.
- *Useful records*. These records are moderately useful for the conduct of ongoing business operations, but will likely not be needed beyond short-term operations. Consequently, a retention period of no more than three years should be adequate. Examples are bank statements, customer correspondence, and operational reports.
- *Important records*. These records are essential to the long-term operations of the business and would be difficult to replace if lost. Consequently, the storage period could be for as long as 10 years. Examples are financial statements and the credit histories of customers.
- *Essential records*. These records are essential to the continuation of the business, and so must be retained in perpetuity. Examples are shareholder records and board minutes.

The duration of a record retention period will depend on a combination of company policy and legal requirements. This means that there is no master retention period that is followed by all organizations, everywhere. Instead, a records retention schedule is custom-designed for each business. The minimum retention period is certainly set by the relevant legal requirements, but an entity may have valid reasons for extending retention periods beyond the legal requirement. The exact retention periods selected will be derived based on the input of several departments, with particular attention to the advice of legal counsel.

When developing a records retention schedule, consideration must be given to not just the total retention period, but also to the periods during which the records will be active and inactive. It is assumed that active records will be accessed regularly, and will need to be stored close by employees. These records will probably be accessed infrequently, and so can be shifted to lower-cost off-site storage for which ready access is more difficult. It is of some importance not to keep records on active status for too long, since this will choke the prime storage locations with records, making it more difficult for employees to access the records they really need.

A sample records retention schedule appears in the following exhibit, showing retention periods for a selection of record types. Human resources and tax-related record retention are addressed later in this section.

Sample Records Retention Schedule

Record Types	Active Period (Years)	Inactive Period (Years)	Total Period (Years)
Accounting and Finance			
Bank statements	2	3	5
Financial statements	3	7	10
General ledger	3	7	10
Payables ledger	2	8	10
Receivables ledger	2	8	10
Corporate			
Board minutes	Permanent	--	Permanent
Capitalization schedule	Permanent	--	Permanent
Corporate bylaws	Permanent	--	Permanent
Operations			
Inventory records	2	3	5
Purchase orders	2	3	5
Purchase requisitions	2	3	5
Selling and Administration			
Customer contracts	5	5	10
Customer credit applications	3	7	10
Customer orders	2	3	5

Human Resources Records Retention Schedule

A variety of legislation has mandated the minimum periods over which human resources records must be maintained. The following table states these intervals, and the minimum employer size for which the storage requirement is mandated.

Human Resources Records Retention Schedule

Record Type	Retention Period	Minimum Employer Size
Affirmative action program documents	2 years	Qualifying federal contractors
Age certification	While employed	No minimum
Benefit payments	3 years	20+ employees
COBRA notice issuances	6 years	20+ employees
COBRA procedures	6 years	20+ employees
Collective bargaining agreements	3 years	No minimum
Compensation records	3 years	20+ employees
Deductions from pay	2 years	No minimum
Disability status	1-2 years	Depends on size
Employee benefit plans	1 year after plan termination	20+ employees
Employment applications	1 year	15+ employees
Employment contracts	3 years	No minimum
Employment test results	1 year	20+ employees
FMLA* disputes documentation	3 years	50+ employees
FMLA* leave dates	3 years	50+ employees
FMLA* notices	3 years	50+ employees
FMLA* premium payments for benefits	3 years	50+ employees
Hazardous materials exposure documentation	30 years	11+ employees
I-9 Form	Later of 3 years or 1 year after employment	4+ employees
Income tax withholding documentation	4 years	No minimum
Injury logs	5 years	11+ employees
Job announcements	1 year	No minimum
Layoffs and recalls	1 year	15+ employees
Minority and female applicant records	3 years	No minimum
Pension plan beneficiary designations	Indefinite	All but governments and churches
Pension plan descriptions and annual reports	6 years	All but governments and churches
Pension plan eligibility documentation	Indefinite	All but governments and churches
Personal information (name, address, social security number, gender, date of birth, occupation, and job classification)	3 years	20+ employees
Polygraph test results and reason for test	3 years	No minimum
Pre-employment records for temporary positions	1 year	20+ employees

Record Type	Retention Period	Minimum Employer Size
Promotions and demotions	1 year	15+ employees
Reasonable accommodation requests	1 year	15+ employees
Records of hours worked	3 years	20+ employees
Records related to discrimination charges	Until resolved	15+ employees
Resumes	1 year	15+ employees
Salary calculations	3 years	No minimum
Tax deductions	3 years	20+ employees
Terminations	1 year	15+ employees
Toxic substance exposure medical exam records	30 years	11+ employees
Training records	1 year	20+ employees
Training records for safety and health topics	3 years	11+ employees
Veteran status	1-2 years	Depends on size
Wage records used to calculate retirement benefits	6 years	All but governments and churches
Work schedules	2 years	No minimum

* Family and Medical Leave Act

State and local laws may mandate longer retention intervals, so periodically check local regulations to see if they override the intervals noted here. Also, these retention periods are only the minimums. It may make sense to retain records for longer periods of time to ensure that the company has an adequate defense in case a lawsuit is filed prior to the expiration of any applicable statute of limitations.

IRS-Mandated Records Retention

The Internal Revenue Service (IRS) requires that an employer retain all records of employment taxes for at least four years. These records should include:

- Employer identification number
- Amounts and dates of all wage, annuity, and pension payments
- Amounts of tips reported to the company by its employees
- Records of allocated tips
- The fair market value of in-kind wages paid
- The names, addresses, social security numbers, and occupations of employees and recipients
- Employee copies of Forms W-2 and W-2c that were returned to the company as undeliverable
- Date of employment for each employee
- Periods for which employees and recipients were paid while absent due to sickness or injury, and the amount and weekly rate of payments made to them

- Copies of employees' and recipients' income tax withholding allowance certificates
- Dates and amounts of tax deposits made by the company and acknowledgement numbers for deposits made
- Copies of returns filed and the related confirmation numbers
- Records of fringe benefits and expense reimbursements provided to employees, including substantiation

An employer must also retain documents for four years that support the information in its annual federal unemployment tax return. This information should include:

- Total wages paid during the calendar year
- Total wages paid during the calendar year that are subject to federal unemployment taxes
- Unemployment tax payments paid to the various state unemployment funds

Record Protection Measures

There are a number of steps that can be taken to protect records. However, some are relatively expensive, so it can make sense to only apply the most extensive records protection steps to the most essential records. Here are a number of record protection measures to consider:

- *Copies*. Create copies of records and store the copies in a separate location.
- *Backups*. Make backups of all computer records and store them offsite. Consider having multiple backup versions that are all stored in different locations. Cloud storage is a viable option.
- *Bank vault*. Store the most critical records in a bank safe deposit box.
- *Fire protection*. Use fire-resistant storage containers. The best containers can maintain an internal temperature below the flash point of paper documents for multiple hours.
- *Humidity protection*. High humidity levels can cause mold, which can destroy records. Store records in an air conditioned room to prevent this. Also, do not store records under overhead pipes, since they could burst, and avoid storage in basement areas that could flood.
- *Pest control*. Certain types of insects (such as termites) can destroy physical records, so regularly treat the records storage area for them.
- *Password protection*. If electronic records are being used, ensure that they are adequately protected by a strong password policy, so that intruders cannot modify or destroy the records.

Record Destruction

When the disposition date of a record is reached, it is scheduled for destruction. This does not mean that the record is simply thrown in the trash. Doing so would allow outsiders to peruse the records and extract confidential information. Instead, records may be shredded, burned, or pulped. The intention is to completely obliterate all of the information contained on the records. The types of shredders that can be used are as follows:

- *Cross-cut.* Shreds documents both vertically and horizontally, which is among the most thorough shredding techniques.
- *Diamond-cut.* Shreds documents both vertically and diagonally, resulting in diamond-shaped pieces. It is quite difficult to reconstruct these pieces.
- *Strip-cut.* Slices documents into strips. This is a faster shredding machine, but it is possible that the strips could be reconstructed.
- *Tear and crush.* Punctures and tears paper, and then crushes it. This device is used for high-volume records destruction.

The process flow when a records disposition date is reached is as follows:

1. Notify the originating department that the records are scheduled for destruction. This gives the department manager a chance to delay or suspend the destruction date. A suspension may be used when there are legal proceedings or audits that require the use of the indicated records. If so, a records hold order is issued to ensure that the relevant records are not destroyed.
2. Obtain a signed authorization to proceed with the record destruction.
3. Witness the record destruction and sign the authorization to indicate that the records were destroyed.
4. Flag the records in the inactive records index to indicate the destruction. This information may instead be stored in a separate destruction file that also indicates the method of destruction.
5. File the record destruction authorization form, in case anyone later needs to verify the paperwork. This can happen when a lawsuit occurs and lawyers want to verify that the records no longer exist.

Records Management Best Practices

There are a number of ways to improve a bloated and disorganized records management system. In this section, we make suggestions that follow these general themes:

- *Document reduction.* Many documents will never be referenced for research purposes, and there is no legal need to retain them. If so, they should either not be allowed into the storage area or pruned from it.
- *Document locations.* Do not force employees to walk an excessive distance to access files. Instead, position storage as close to them as possible.
- *Document indexing and sorting.* Make it as easy as possible to locate files. Also, pre-sorting records prior to filing makes the filing process more efficient.
- *Document consolidation.* Combine files under certain circumstances, so that related records are not positioned in multiple locations.

These themes are expanded upon through the remainder of this section.

Report Purge

A business may have a large number of reports that are issued on a daily, weekly, or monthly basis. While useful from an operational perspective, there may not be a good reason to retain them for very long. A good records management opportunity is to purge all of these reports once the fiscal year has been completed, but to keep the year-end reports. A company may be want to retain this year-end information for several years to come, and so may need to keep these supporting documents on hand, especially if there is to be a financial or operational comparison to the results in prior years.

Copy Elimination

In a few businesses, it is still a common procedure to print multiple copies of some documents, such as customer invoices, and keep several versions for internal filing. For example, one copy may be filed by customer name, while another copy is filed by invoice number. Since all businesses of any size have software that can bring up on-line versions of almost any document, there is little point in printing and filing a document version just so that someone can manually access the same information. Consequently, no additional document copy should ever be printed and stored.

Individual Folder Creation Policy

The general folder in a filing system can become stuffed with an excessive number of miscellaneous records. This can make it difficult to properly file records into this folder, as well as to locate records within it. To keep the amount of records in the general folder at a manageable level, adopt a policy that an individual folder will be created once a certain number of records have piled up in the general folder that relate to a correspondent. For example, once the number of invoices issued to A.B. Smith & Sons exceeds five records, extract the records from the general folder and move them into an individual folder.

To make this policy work, establish a periodic date (perhaps quarterly), when all general folders are examined to see if record totals have exceeded the established corporate policy. This practice is more likely to be followed if the date selected is not in the middle of some other major activity that will consume the attention of the staff, such as the annual audit.

Record Pre-Sorting

It can be quite helpful to pre-sort a stack of documents before filing. This may involve just sorting within a letter of the alphabet or by topic, without attempting to achieve a more perfect level of sorting between individual documents. By doing so, a person engaged in filing will be able to move in one direction through the filing system while filing records approximately in sequence. This is a substantial improvement over a situation in which records have not been pre-sorted, which requires a filer to move back and forth through the filing area to file each unsorted record. For example, unsorted records might require a person to first file a document in a filing cabinet that houses all letter M records, then file a document in the A filing cabinet, and then switch to the Y filing cabinet. If the records had been pre-sorted, the person could have filed all A documents first, then moved to the B filing cabinet, and so forth.

Filing Cabinet Locations

A typical filing scenario is for documents to be stored in a row of filing cabinets in one part of a department's work area. When documents are consolidated in this fashion, travel times to and from the cabinets are only optimized for those people working close to the cabinets. Those working at the other end of the department will find that they are spending an inordinate amount of time walking back and forth between document storage and their offices.

A better approach is to replace a single large storage area with a number of smaller locations that are situated in the center of the areas where they are most needed. For example:

- Move all current supplier files into the accounts payable area
- Move the billing and collections staffs close together and park the current customer files in the middle of this group
- Move current payroll files into the payroll manager's office, and ensure that the office door is locked, to provide extra security for the files

Filing Carts

Even if filing cabinets are moved close to those employees most likely to use them, the staff must still stand up and walk to the cabinets, which means that there is still travel time to be rooted out of the system.

A possible solution is to provide the heavier users of files with mobile office carts. They can then shift any documents they need from fixed storage locations into the carts, and roll the carts to where they are working. If employees switch to different workstations during the day, they can just move the carts along with them.

> **Tip:** The only issue with office carts is that they can clutter up the work area, so only buy them in a size that can be readily rolled underneath a work surface to get them out of the way.

Longer Storage Intervals

The standard practice at the end of a fiscal year is to move all files from the preceding year into inactive storage and prepare a set of new folders in which to store information for the new year. For example, customer billing files and supplier invoice files are routinely moved off-site in this manner. The problem with this approach is that the outgoing files may contain documents that are only a few weeks or months old (e.g., from the end of the last fiscal year) and which the clerical staff will almost certainly need to reference over the next few months, as the inevitable research questions arise.

There are two ways to deal with this issue:

- Keep files on hand for both the old and new fiscal years in the same filing cabinets, so that the files are available for both. Then, after the need for the older files diminishes (probably in about 90 days), move the older files to archival storage. This approach has the advantage of not taking up too much additional on-site storage space, and should be sufficient for most research issues.
- Retain information on-site for two years, rather than one year. Then extract the oldest year of records from the files and move them to archival storage. This approach requires twice the amount of on-site storage space, but has the advantage of being able to address essentially all research issues. Any visits to archival storage should be extremely rare, which makes it possible to move the off-site storage area further away to take advantage of lower-cost storage space.

Storage Improvements

Employees usually do quite a good job of labeling the current files that are located on-site. However, this discipline typically breaks down when the files are moved to inactive storage. Employees have a disturbing habit of throwing files into boxes, palletizing the boxes, and sticking them on a distant shelf in the warehouse – and probably under a sprinkler head. Instead, consider the following storage improvements:

- *Consistent contents.* Do not jumble documents into a storage box. Instead, ensure that material is consistently filed, such as putting all bank records in one or a set of boxes. This may require the use of additional boxes.
- *Consistent boxes.* Use the same type of box for all storage. When all boxes are identical, the cubic volume of the storage area can be most efficiently utilized, and also results in better stacking. These boxes should have a minimum crush weight of 200 pounds, to prevent box damage when they are stacked.
- *Detailed content labeling.* Carefully identify everything in a box and state the contents clearly on the outside of the box.
- *Accessible storage.* Reserve a storage room in which storage racks are set up at no more than head height, and with readily accessible tables on which storage boxes can be opened.
- *Labels face outward.* Store all boxes in the storage racks so that the labeled end of each box is facing outward, with no additional boxes hidden behind them.
- *Functional storage layout.* Cluster together storage boxes containing similar document types (such as all supplier records), and in alphabetical order within these clusters.

Tip: Be sure to segregate essential records (such as legal documents and property title documents) from those files that will eventually be destroyed. Keep the essential records in an entirely separate location, in fireproof and locked cabinets.

Though these steps certainly take more time to complete, and may require additional storage boxes and storage space, the result should be vastly less research time to locate documents that have been placed in inactive storage.

Document Imaging

There may be situations where a business must deal with massive amounts of paperwork, or where documents cannot be stored near employees, or where several clerks may need access to the same document at the same time. A document imaging system can resolve these problems.

Document imaging involves scanning documents as they arrive at the company, assigning an index number to the images, and storing them in a high-volume storage device. The source documents are then sent to inactive storage. With document imaging in place, there is no need for any document storage in higher-cost office space. Also, many people can access the same image at the same time on their computer terminals. Thus, document imaging can be an excellent technology solution to the old problem of dealing with too much paper.

However, there are a number of issues with document imaging that make it an effective solution only in certain situations. First, there needs to be a system in place for scanning documents, which will require additional clerical help. Alternatively, there are suppliers to which paperwork can be routed, who will digitize documents on the company's behalf. Also, if documents are not properly indexed in the imaging system, they can be quite difficult to find. And third, the cost of the system's software and hardware can be excessive for a smaller business.

Document imaging is least practical where the number of employees is relatively small, and they are already centrally located with the relevant records nearby. Conversely, it may be an excellent solution if there are many records, the department is large, and there is an ongoing need to access a large number of records.

Document Consolidation and Clarification

On rare occasions, a supplier or customer will change its name. While cross-referencing can be used in the filing system to trace back to documents filed under the original name, an alternative is to move all records under the new name. This approach is most effective when there are relatively few documents under the original name; it will result in fewer multi-location searches. If this approach is used, it will be necessary to create a cross-reference that leads from the old name to the new name.

It is quite easy for the number of records to completely overwhelm a folder. When this is the case, documents can be damaged and it is more likely that documents will not be sorted correctly. Both issues can make it more difficult to access information. To eliminate these issues, prepare additional folders for the same correspondent, and label them in chronological order.

For example, a plethora of records for customer A.B. Smith could result in the following set of four consecutive folders:

1. A.B. Smith – Jan.-Mar.
2. A.B. Smith – Apr.-Jun.
3. A.B. Smith – Jul.-Sep.
4. A.B. Smith – Oct.-Dec.

The Tickler File

A tickler file is a chronological sorting of information that is intended to reminder a user when to take certain actions. The layout of a tickler file is a set of folders numbered for each date in the current month, followed by 12 folders that represent all of the months in a year. At the start of each month, notes are inserted into the daily folders to remind users of actions to take during certain days. Once the month has been completed, all notes are cleared from the daily folders, and replaced by notes from the next month's folder.

While a tickler file might appear to be nothing more than a manual reminder system, it can also temporarily store records. For example, a business license renewal reminder could be kept in a tickler file, as a reminder to renew the license as of a certain date. Once the reminder item is completed, the related record is moved from the tickler file to the main storage area.

Mis-Filing Solutions

There are ways to minimize the amount of record mis-filings. Consider the following approaches:

- *Color coding.* Use a specific color for each letter of the alphabet on all tabs. For example, every folder beginning with the letter "A" has a blue color. With this color coding in place, it will be immediately apparent if an "A" folder is filed anywhere else in the storage system.
- *Numeric coding.* When numbers are assigned to records instead of names or subjects, it is easier to find the records when they have been mis-filed, since it will be obvious when they are out of sequence.
- *Missing record tracking system.* Whenever a record goes missing, mark it down in a log, and routinely examine the log for patterns. It is quite possible that a procedure is not being followed, or errors can be traced back to a specific individual, in which case additional training can be used to minimize the ongoing rate of mis-filings.

There are also several techniques for locating missing records, which can be combined into a general search routine. They are:

1. *Look around the folder.* This means looking between the folders on either side of the correct folder, as well as underneath the folder. In the latter case, a

record might have been inserted between two folders, and then slid underneath.

2. *Look within the folder.* Open the correct folder and search all the way through it, on the assumption that the record was not inserted in the correct chronological order.

3. *Look in the general folder.* If the person filing the record did not see an individual folder, the next logical place to file the record would be in the general folder for the relevant alphabet letter.

4. *Look for name transpositions.* A two-part name might have been filed under a transposed name. For example, the name of Quincy Jones might have been filed under Jones Quincy.

5. *Look under alternate indexing units.* The record might have been filed based on its second or third (or later) indexing unit, so look in those areas.

6. *Ask.* After the preceding approaches have been used, put out a general request to see if anyone has the record in their work area. If so, there needs to be a discussion about the proper usage of OUT indicators (see the Record Storage Supplies section).

Practices to Avoid

It may be tempting to examine each file just before sending it to inactive storage, and prune out redundant or otherwise unnecessary documents. This is not necessary, since the cost of inactive storage is relatively inexpensive, and saving a few boxes and the cost of a few extra square feet of storage is not worthwhile. Furthermore, there is a risk of inadvertently throwing away key documents. Instead, just transfer all designated files to inactive storage in bulk.

Analysis of Records Management Best Practices

The ultimate records management system involves document imaging, since records are permanently available to anyone who has access to a computer. However, it is an expensive option, so a mix of the other recommendations in this section can be used to arrive at a suitable operation that is not so technologically advanced. In particular, we find that moving filing cabinets to employee locations is one of the simpler options, since it nearly eliminates employee travel times. Consider using the other suggestions if they are cost-effective.

Summary

There are many component parts to a records management system, and they must all work together in order to arrive at a system that works in the most optimal manner. This means focusing on every aspect of how an organization operates, and then tailoring the underlying system to meet the needs of the business. For example, if the core competency of a business is exquisite customer service, then it may be necessary to install a document imaging system, irrespective of the cost, so that employees can call up customer records at their desks while talking to customers on the phone.

Conversely, if a business operates on a philosophy of high volume and low costs, every effort will be made to drive down records management costs, with customer service probably being relegated to a minor consideration. Thus, when perusing the variety of suggestions in this chapter, keep in mind how they will fit into the mode of operation of the business.

Chapter 4
Electronic Records Management

Introduction

The preceding discussion of records management has concentrated on the handling of physical records. However, the bulk of the records maintained by an organization may be electronic, rather than physical. If so, there are a number of additional considerations that apply to the management, safety, retention, and destruction of these records, which we address in the following sections.

Electronic Records Management

The preceding discussion of records management in a physical records environment does not necessarily translate into an electronic records management system. There are multiple ways to search for records within an electronic environment. In the following sub-sections, we describe the use of directories and metadata to organize electronic records. We also note the use of databases to store similar types of data in a consistent manner.

Directories

When records are filed electronically, they are stored within directories. A directory is a subdivision of storage space that is set aside by the operating system of a computer. A directory may be further sub-divided into a sub-directory, which in turn may be sub-divided further. The result can be a deeply layered directory structure. A sample directory structure follows.

Sample Directory Structure

Top Level Directory	Second Level Directory	Third Level Directory	Fourth Level Directory	Fifth Level Directory
Accounting				
	Budget			
		Engineering		
			Staff Budget	
				Headcount Budget

The intent behind using a multi-layered directory structure is to make it easier to locate files. The directory structure can be optimized by following these rules:

- *Clarify directory names.* Ensure that each directory name is unique and clearly describes all files stored within it. Otherwise, a user may be faced with a search through several different directories that are all peripherally related.
- *Clarify file names.* Operating systems allow for lengthy file names, so make use of this feature and enter as much information into a file name as is needed to fully identify it. Conversely, avoid abbreviations, since they are difficult to interpret.
- *Optimize directory levels.* Include a sufficient number of nested directories to optimize record searches, without using so many that a user will be lost among the many choices.

Over time, the number of files that can accumulate within a directory structure can become overwhelming, making it more difficult to search for files. To mitigate the level of this inefficiency, set a date on which users are requested to examine their files and shift them into a different directory structure that is intended for long-term storage.

Metadata

Metadata is data that describes other data. From a records management perspective, the key benefit of metadata is that it assists in locating records. Examples of the metadata that might be associated with a record are:

- *Unique document identification.* This may be a numeric value from the entity's filing system that is assigned to the document.
- *Title of the record.* This is the stated name of the document.
- *Subject of the record.* This is a brief description of the document.
- *Author of the record.* This is the name of the person who created the document.
- *Owning department.* This is the name of the department that has control over the document; usually the department in which it was created.
- *Date of origination.* This is the date on which the document was created.
- *Holding period.* This is the amount of time that the document is to be held prior to disposition.
- *Security level.* This is the security level assigned to the document, based on its confidentiality and how critical it is to the operations of the business.

For example, if metadata were created for a movie, it could include the name of the movie, its date of release, the film format, the type of movie, the name of the director, and the names of the actors.

Metadata is either manually or automatically generated when a record is created. The computer system can then search through the metadata for all of the records stored in the system, and can locate records based on any element of the metadata. Metadata contains more data than a simple file name, so it is more likely to pinpoint a record than a file name search.

If it is necessary to include e-mails in a records management system, metadata should be created for these messages, to improve the probability that they can be retrieved at a later date.

Databases

The prior discussion of directories and metadata can be applied to a broad range of record types. A more organized approach to electronic records management is the database. A *database* is a systematically organized repository of indexed information. A database contains records, which are comprised of fields. Each field contains a set of characters that are treated as a unit of information. For example, a supplier record contains fields for the name of each supplier, its address, contact information, and taxpayer identification number. Because of the rigid structure of this field-record system, an organization can accumulate a large amount of consistent information relating to specific areas of the business. In addition, the database software indexes the entire database based on a unique identifier that is included in each record, so that information can be retrieved based on a database search.

A database is particularly useful for sorting information in multiple ways. For example, an inventory database can be sorted by warehouse location code, so that an inventory count can be conducted. Or, the same database can be re-sorted by extended valuation, to see if any inventory items have been assigned incorrect costs or units of measure.

Given the capabilities of a database, an organization should strive to maintain as much of its information as possible in a formal database. The most extensive database system is the enterprise resource planning (ERP) system. This is an integrated software package that supports all of a company's functional areas. Thus, it can handle the transactional requirements of the accounting, customer service, manufacturing, sales, warehousing, and other departments. Many ERP systems also accept data from a company's customers and suppliers for supply chain management purposes, so that the system surpasses the traditional boundaries of a corporation.

The great advantage of an ERP system is that *all* corporate data is integrated, so data is only entered into the system once (as opposed to the "silo" approach, where information is entered into the separate software packages used by each department). With an integrated ERP system, companies find that their transaction error rates decline, while many tasks that formerly required manual effort are now entirely automated. Also, subject to security issues, employees can access information in other departments that was previously difficult to obtain, or only with the help of special programming by the IT department.

The downside of an ERP system is its extreme complexity. The software requires a great deal of time to set up, as well as to convert a company's existing data into it. Also, because ERP systems can only be configured in a limited number of ways, most companies will find that they must alter their operating procedures to fit the software, rather than altering the software to fit their procedures. These changes call for a large training expenditure, and may result in resistance from those employees accustomed to the old system. These issues call for an implementation budget in the millions of dollars, and several years of intensive effort to complete.

A less-expensive alternative to an ERP system is to assemble only those software modules from various software vendors that are considered most crucial to company operations, and create custom interfaces to transfer information between the modules. This approach does not provide a comprehensive, company-wide solution and usually requires the updating of interfaces whenever a software upgrade is installed. However, it allows for the use of industry-specific modules that closely fit the needs of a business. This approach works best for smaller organizations that cannot afford a comprehensive ERP solution.

Electronic Media

Electronic media come in a variety of types, each with its own advantages and disadvantages in relation to how they can be used for records management. In the following bullet points, we briefly note the characteristics of each one:

- *Cloud storage.* This is a service that allows users to store and manage data on remote servers accessed via the internet. Key characteristics include exceptional scalability, accessibility from anywhere with an Internet connection, cost-effectiveness, and (usually) a high degree of reliability.
- *Magnetic media – hard drive.* This is a metal platter with magnetic properties that allow data to be stored on it. Hard drives are subject to failure because they spin at high speeds, and so require regular backups.
- *Magnetic media – tape.* This is a tape with a magnetized coating, on which data can be stored. Tapes can store large amounts of information, but read times are quite slow.
- *Optical media.* This is a plastic disc on which information is digitally encoded with a laser. Data can be stored permanently on optical media. It is considered safe for long-term storage.
- *Solid state media.* This is one or more flash memory chips on which information is stored, even when there is no power. Data access is extremely fast, and a large amount can be stored in quite a small amount of physical space. Failure rates are low, since there are no moving parts. However, this is the most expensive storage method.

Electronic Records

The most common elements of an electronic records management system are files generated by a database program, electronic documents, and electronic spreadsheets. There are usually systems in place for storing these files. However, there are also a number of messages that could be classified as records, and which fall outside of the normal records management system. These include e-mails, text messages, tweets, podcasts, blog posts, and social media posts. Users need to decide which of these items are to be classified as records, and then file them in the appropriate directory as indicated by the nature of the underlying information.

Electronic records that should have been deleted can be damaging to a business when they are uncovered during a legal discovery process as part of a lawsuit. To minimize this risk, use the following procedures to ensure that records are fully eliminated from the system once their retention periods have ended:

- Issue periodic reminders to users to purge their e-mails at regular intervals.
- Set a maximum e-mail storage level for each user, so that they are forced to purge some e-mails in order to create sufficient space for the storage of more e-mails.
- Regularly communicate to employees the need to avoid stating anything in an electronic message that could later be used in court.

Electronic Records Safety

A firm may have the bulk of its information stored in electronic records, so if these records are destroyed, the organization may not be able to continue in business. Consequently, it is mandatory to adopt a number of measures to protect these records. Here are several protective actions to consider:

- *Backups*. Backup all electronic records multiple times, and store each version in a different location in order to mitigate the risk of loss. There are several variations on this concept, which are:
  - *Full backup*. Involves a complete backup of all files, which takes longer to complete. However, restorations of the data can be relatively fast.
  - *Incremental backup*. Only backs up data that has been modified since the last backup, which reduces the backup time. However, restorations can take longer, since several layers of backups may need to be accessed.
  - *Mirror backup*. Makes a complete backup the first time, and incremental backups thereafter. This results in a fast backup as well as a fast restoration.
  - *Cloud*. A backup system automatically monitors files from an offsite location and incrementally updates backed up files as they are added or changed. This results in up-to-date backups at all times, though the restore process can be slow.

- *Controlled access*. Lock all access doors leading to computer storage equipment, and require keypad, biometric, or badge access through these doors.
- *Controlled environment*. Store electronic media away from heat sources, high humidity environments, electromagnetic sources, and direct sunlight, all of which can damage them. A filtered and air conditioned environment works best.
- *Encryption*. Data can be scrambled using encryption, so that it can only be read by someone with the deciphering key. Thus, even if records are stolen, they cannot be read.

- *Firewalls*. Install firewalls between the outside world and the organization's computer systems, to keep computer viruses from accessing and destroying or stealing electronic records. A firewall is a filter that blocks certain types of data.
- *Security policy*. Allow employees access only to those records that they need. Also, require password access to electronic records, and mandate that these passwords be changed on a regular basis.
- *Surge protectors*. Install surge protectors in the power feeds for all electronic equipment, so that the equipment will not be damaged by power fluctuations.
- *Virus detection*. Install virus detection software that scans for and removes any viruses found in a computer.

Electronic Records Retention and Destruction

The same procedures used for the retention of physical records apply to electronic records. However, a key difference is that the quality of some types of electronic storage media may break down over time. This is a particular concern for magnetic storage media. In cases where such media is being employed for record storage, copy the records onto a longer-term storage medium before sending it to inactive storage. The basic rule to observe is that the stable life expectancy of the storage media should match or exceed the planned retention period of a document.

An additional concern is that media formats and sizes change over time, and it may become more difficult to find any equipment to read the older media. For example, 5.25" floppy disks were replaced by 3.5" disks, which were replaced by compact discs – and compact discs are now appearing in increasing levels of storage density. Consequently, it may be necessary to periodically copy records onto the newest storage media. Because of this issue, it makes sense to maintain an index of electronic records that includes the storage media being used; the records manager can then sort the index based on a certain type of storage media that is now considered to be at risk, and concentrate on shifting those records onto the newest storage media.

When it is time to destroy an electronic record, consider taking additional steps to ensure that the information has been completely eliminated. For example, once a file has been deleted, overwrite the space on the storage disk that had been occupied by the file. Also, consider applying a strong magnetic field to magnetic storage media in order to wipe out any information stored on them. Another option is to physically destroy the storage media; this is most practical for storage tapes and discs, as well as USB flash drives.

Catastrophic Damage Risk

A business may maintain all of its information technology (IT) equipment, software, and staff at a single location. This may be an efficient way to run the department, especially when the IT group is located on the premises with the rest of the company. However, if the building is destroyed or damaged, perhaps by a tornado or flooding, the organization's entire IT capability has just been destroyed, along with its electronic records. There are several partial and more extensive ways to reduce this risk, which are:

- *Backup data off-site.* It can be quite useful to arrange for automatic backups of electronic data to a cloud data center. By doing so, the data can be downloaded back to the company once the period of danger has passed and there are computers available to accept the download. Taking this step might also provide an incentive for a business to digitize a larger proportion of its paper records, so that this information can also be stored in the cloud.
- *Install backup power supplies.* Provide all key computer equipment with uninterruptible power supplies. Doing so keeps the equipment operational until it can be shut down in an orderly manner.
- *Enforce a backup procedure.* Test the automated data backup system to ensure that data is indeed being backed up at the designated times.
- *Elevate equipment.* Position as much computer and other electrical equipment as possible above ground, to reduce the risk of water damage.
- *Locate IT separately.* It can make sense to construct a separate facility for the IT group that is located well away from any locations prone to natural disasters.
- *Maintain a hot site.* The company can rent a backup IT facility that is maintained by a third party, or maintain its own backup site. This approach is most effective if the IT staff practices transitioning over to the backup facility on a regular basis.
- *Outsource systems.* It may be possible to use cloud-based solutions that are maintained by third parties. A localized disaster does not impact these providers, so employees can continue to access the systems from alternate locations, as long as they have Internet access.

The preventive actions noted here can be assembled into a formal disaster recovery plan. This plan itemizes how records will be handled during a catastrophic damage incident, as well as how a recovery will be completed. The plan may note several types of incidents, and the recovery procedures associated with each one. For example, there could be separate recovery procedures if there is water damage, a prolonged power outage, or a terrorist attack.

A disaster recovery plan should focus on several key areas to ensure that records are recovered as completely and as soon as possible. These areas include:

- *Response personnel.* Those positions responsible for taking action are identified, and their responsibilities are stated.
- *Recovery priorities.* The plan notes which records are the most critical to the ongoing work of the organization, so that these records will be recovered first.
- *Response procedures.* Procedures specifically state the steps to be followed to mitigate damage and recover systems in an orderly manner.
- *Off-site recovery assistance.* The plan lists all suppliers that can assist with a recovery, including their contact information.

Any disaster recovery plan must be tested at intervals to ensure that it is workable. Periodic tests may uncover flaws in the plan, while also giving employees practice in their assigned tasks.

Summary

Of particular concern in an electronic records management system is unauthorized access to records. If this happens, vital records can be extracted and used by competitors or simply be exposed to the world – either situation can have devastating results. To minimize this risk, implement the security recommendations noted in this chapter. In addition, call in a security specialist to examine the company's electronic records management systems, to spot possible problems and recommend changes. This should be an ongoing concern, since the ability of hackers to attack systems continues to improve.

Glossary

A

Accession log. A logbook in which is maintained a serial listing of every number issued in a numeric records management system.

Active record. A record that is regularly accessed by users.

D

Direct access. A filing system in which an index is not needed to search for a record.

Directory. A subdivision of storage space that is set aside by the operating system of a computer.

Document imaging. A document scanning, indexing, storage, and retrieval system that scans paper documents and stores the image in an electronic format.

E

External records. Records containing information that is intended for use outside of the entity.

F

Filing segment. The name under which a record is both stored and later requested by users.

Folder. A cardboard container that holds the records in a file.

Follower block. A metal plate at the back of a file drawer that can be adjusted to reduce the effective length of the drawer.

G

General folder. A folder that contains records involving small volumes, where there is no need for a specially-designated folder.

H

Hanging folder. A folder that is used to store records within each drawer of a filing cabinet.

I

Inactive record. A record that is rarely accessed by users.

Indexing order. The order in which the units of a filing segment are considered for record storage.

Indexing rules. The system of markings used to present the ordering of filing segments.

Indexing units. The words that comprise a filing segment.

Indirect access. A two-step process of first looking up a subject in an index, and then going to the records management system to access the applicable folder.

Individual folder. A folder that stores only the records for a specific correspondent.

Information governance. The system of policies and procedures that provides structure to a records management system.

Internal records. Records that are needed to operate a business.

M

Metadata. Data that describes other data.

O

OUT indicator. A sheet or folder that indicates the location of records that have been removed from storage.

R

Record. Stored information used as evidence and information, and which has value by being retained for a certain period of time.

Records management. The systematic administration of records for their entire life cycle, beginning with their creation or receipt and extending through their classification, use, filing, retention, storage, and eventual disposition.

Reference record. Records that are used to support operational decisions occurring at longer intervals than ongoing daily operations.

S

Score marks. Indented lines along the bottom edge of a folder that can be folded along to expand the storage capacity of the folder.

T

Tab. A projection that rises above the edge of a folder or guide, and which contains indexing information.

Transaction record. Records that are used in the conduct of a firm's daily operations, usually created with standard forms.

Index